GRAND ILLUSIONS
New Decorating

Trafalgar Square Publishing

GRAND ILLUSIONS
New Decorating

TECHNIQUES, IDEAS & INSPIRATION FOR CREATING A FRESH LOOK

Nick Ronald and David Roberts
Special Photography by David Downie

Trafalgar Square Publishing

747

First published in the United States of America
in 1998 by Trafalgar Square Publishing
North Pomfret, Vermont 05053

Printed and bound in Italy

ISBN 1-57076-122-1

Library of Congress Catalog Card Number: 98-84278

Art direction: Meryl Lloyd
Design: Alison Shackleton
Editors: Emma Callery, Jo Copestick
Photography: David Downie
Photographic Styling: Meryl Lloyd, Nick Ronald

1 3 5 7 9 10 8 6 4 2

contents

the well-travelled decorator

New Decorating is every bit as much about discovering the senses as it is about the decorating styles derived from around the world that are explored within these pages. In this rapidly moving and ever-changing world, decorating is becoming an aesthetic experience rather than some cosmetic colour chart for change – after all, travel is a sensory experience and a global palette is a feast for all the senses.

The idea of a well-travelled decorator need not be taken literally, nor should the suggestions contained in this book. Rather, we offer ideas and inspiration from around this planet, to be plundered at will. To develop your own inimitable style, take from it what you will, mix with it what you wish. To help you achieve this, at the start of every chapter we have chosen some images to inspire you, followed by elements of the style. These are tangible ideas to consider so that you can then go ahead and create your own style: a visual pot pourri if you like.

As ever, the projects are innovative and have been tried and tested by us to ensure that the results are always believably professional, rather than trivial and lightweight. It is our intrinsic belief that most people can achieve most things, given the time and guidance.

With such lofty ideals, it is no surprise that, in our view, building a home is not something which can be hurried. It needs to evolve naturally and these days has a lot more to do with rejuvenating rather than replacing, making the most of what you have and, above all, enjoying it on every level. We do hope that this book will go some way towards helping you achieve this goal.

global influences

At some time in our lives we have all experienced that feeling of being totally captivated by a place. It could be as simple as the hedonistic delights of a sun-drenched Greek island, the heady atmosphere of the kasbah, or the misty hue of some deep and mysterious Norwegian fjord. We are talking romantic, of course.

But without a doubt, travel broadens the palette as well as the mind, and global influences pervade daily life. Take a look at the food you eat, the clothes you wear, and the music you listen to. Such a broad ranging view of life explains the rise of ancient sciences and alternative medicines it is little wonder that is has had an impact on interior design and decoration, also.

Thankfully, few places on the planet are more than a flight or two away and, in most cases, air travel has never been better value. More importantly, though, and thanks to the absolute wealth of stunning photography now available in magazines, books and Sunday supplements, inspiration is just around the corner. Going global means an ever-increasing access to different ideas and concepts. There is already a very strong Asian influence creeping into modern Western interior design, while the boundaries of the Mediterranean, Mexico and North Africa are merging all the time.

For the consumer, Global Shopping is that much easier, too. Take the fact that Indian and Mexican furniture is readily available in most department stores – an Indian thakat table is now almost as ubiquitous as, say, a farmhouse pine table. Now that really is global and just five short years ago was almost unthinkable. To be quite honest, though, something quite abstract can trigger off a whole flurry of ideas. We can be sufficiently moved at Grand Illusions by just one single image to create a whole new theme, or source a range of products. The image can also lead us on to develop a new paint colour. It really is all part and parcel of the Learning to See philosophy discussed on page 12.

But global influences are not to be taken literally which is why, when conceiving this book, we almost hesitated lest we should confuse and be misunderstood. As we planned the projects that we are featuring in the book, we discovered that many of them would happily sit in at least one or more of the other sections. For example, the faux stone floor with a painted border from Shades of White that is on pages 40-3 would look just as meaningful in the Mediterranean and Spice chapters. We found that colours, too, cross borders. For example, mustard yellow works as well in a Scandinavian scheme as it does in a Provençal one.

Whatever your passions and whatever your inspirations, fuse them together to form an eclectic mix. Take the elements of the style rather than seeking to emulate it in its entirety. Take the essence rather than the whole recipe and then let it evolve naturally. Follow your instincts and you will create an individual statement. Even better, it is your individual statement.

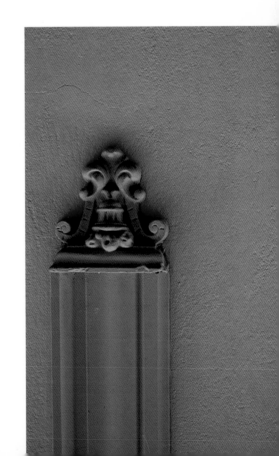

learning to see

In his book *Zona Home*, an American retailer, Louis Sagar, talks at great length about how objects or possessions need to have an enigmatic quality, a soul or energy if you like. He calls it 'Learning to See'. For what it's worth, we think he is absolutely right and it is a subject very close to our hearts. This may sound vaguely pretentious, but it explains why we trawl through literally hundreds, or possibly thousands, of products every year to find a handful that we believe are appropriate for our shops. It is not just a question of taste.

Learning to See is the reasoning that explains why sometimes you are inexplicably drawn to a particular piece and why it becomes a 'must-have' rather than a victim of some 'shop-until-you-drop' experience. These are the very things that should be allowed space in your home.

Take the fireplace in the picture overleaf – it started life as a huge picture frame (and very hideous it was too). We saw it lying discarded in a local junk shop and curiously kept returning to it day after day until we eventually succumbed to the inevitable, finally realizing that it was meant to be. We could see that beyond its initial appearance it had character and spirit. Years later it is still a focal point in our home and something from which we derive great pleasure.

To practise this theory, though, is a process of trial and error and requires discipline if you are to avoid a sea of eclectic clutter. It is also critically important never to lose your sense of spontaneity or fun. Once grasped, however, Learning to See will be your essential guide to decorating, leading the way towards developing and sustaining a cohesive style. With this passion, the 'must-haves' of today will become the heirlooms of tomorrow.

creating atmosphere

There is no doubt that *New Decorating* is an aesthetic experience. It is a veritable feast for all the senses. It is about creating a personal atmosphere or aura. Your home is as personal as your signature and while it is important to have our own private sanctuary, great comfort and pleasure can be derived from the ways in which we choose to communicate this aura to our friends and relatives. Performed well, good communication sparks curiosity and enchantment in our visitors. This in turn leads to invigorating conversation – the very act of sharing enhances the feeling of pleasure.

That is exactly what we do in our shops, or should I say, try to do. By building themes and stories, we aim to spike the imagination of our customers and provide formats for them to copy in their homes. Here are a few simple guidelines to help you ensure that your home is a feast for the senses, evoking a relaxing, peaceful atmosphere.

To hear

To strive for a broad perspective in your choice of music is a healthy objective and the best way of reaching this goal is to experiment. Build up a wide playlist that includes a catholic mix of jazz, classical and contemporary, and try substituting music for television. Background music is wonderfully evocative and is quite perfect for those contemplatory moments.

To smell

Given that not all of life's aromas are pleasant ones, make sure your home is fresh and aromatic with plenty of fresh air circulating throughout the house. Top this up with a layering of other fragrances such as pot pourri, room sprays, essential oils, light-bulb rings and scented candles.

To taste

View your daily meal as a celebration rather than a chore to get through - savour the moment. This is easier said than done in some cases we know, but it should be an important aspiration nevertheless. Take time to celebrate and mark the small things in life.

To touch

Textures are equally important so plan to combine them and mix them - on the walls and on the floors. For maximum effect, seek to mix modern with old and rough with smooth.

To see

Fresh flowers bring natural life and colour into a room - and sometimes perfume, too. They can be expensive, so use flowers that are in season and there is not necessarily any need to buy masses of them at one time. Instead, use a simple bunch or single stem, rather than creating a formal arrangement, and then place them in your favourite jug or vase in a prominent place. Buy them regularly and not as a treat.

capturing light

Light is the single most important factor when decorating or creating a home. Given the recent explosion of specialist paints, offering all manner of evocatively named exotic colours, you could be forgiven for thinking that a can of, say, Santorini Blue used as a border on a white-washed house, is all that is required to transport your home to some idyllic Greek island. You would, of course - and somewhat sadly - be misguided in your belief as you would still be firmly based just where you always have been.

Mediterranean colours, especially when used in combination, can look very sad and dull in Northern light. The honourable exceptions are blues which occasionally, when used in isolation, can be fine; and muted earth tones. So why do Mediterranean colours not work elsewhere? To establish that, you first have to understand how natural light works and how it varies significantly in different locations throughout the world. All light is made up of many different colours, which when fused together make white light or daylight - that Greek light we all seek is light in its purest form. Further north, light moves more and more towards the blue end of the scale and lacks vibrancy. It is softer, greyer and actually far more subtle than the dazzling, sometimes bleaching, glare of the Mediterranean.

This then explains why colours from the blue family, whether neat or toned down with white, or colours that contain blue as a major component (like greens or purples, for example), always work well in a northern interior. Similarly, earth colours such as yellow ochre, terracotta or burnt umber always look good in these areas, as the light brings out the greyish tones that are within them.

When you are decorating a room, the amount of available natural light is a key factor. The more windows you have, the better. More importantly, though, ensure that you are able to maximize daylight during the day, yet minimalize intrusion and maintain privacy at night. Simple blinds, sheers and frosted glass are all modern ways of dealing with this problem. If you cannot increase the amount of natural light in your home, make the most of what you've got with mirrors and glass. Without sufficient light, life can be depressing or dull.

A stimulating environment also needs variation of tone, texture and shadows - what might be fine for the winter months could need a little tweaking in the summer. For example, at home we use warm red lampshades in the winter months and change them for cooler, cream ones in the summertime. Avoid blanket overhead lighting and use downlighters with a dimmer control to create an ambient light where necessary - but remember that not all rooms need it. An element of task lighting is essential for reading or working by and this can be provided by lamps or spotlights; the more light sources there are in a room, the better. Finally, plan for some emotional mood lighting to encourage a sense of relaxation and intimacy. For this, use diffused lighting, paper shades, frosted night-lights and votives, and standard lamps - or, best of all, candles.

feng shui

There is no doubt that re-arranging your possessions in a new combination is one of life's great satisfactions. It creates a revived sense of order and in turn makes a perceptible difference to your life. In the world according to feng shui, this rids the house of bad or stale *ch'i*, creating new paths of energy in the same way you would if you loudly clapped your hands on entering a room.

Feng shui is the Chinese study of energy, or *ch'i*, and its relationship to physical environments. It was once a closely guarded secret in ancient China, used to sustain the good fortune of the royal court. It first came to the attention of the Western world about twenty years ago, when certain new Hong Kong skyscrapers were built in accordance with this discipline.

These days, people practise feng shui to enlighten, harmonize and clarify their lives - by determining the natural rhythms of energy that have a daily effect. Here are some of the basic beliefs:

• Use all five of your senses to create a beautiful home or workplace.

• Balance the elements of a room, light with dark, soft with hard, rough with smooth.

• Get rid of clutter, keeping only things that are essential or of personal value to you.

• Avoid sleeping or working in the energy path of a doorway or under ceiling beams as the turbulence of the *ch'i* will interrupt your concentration or peace of mind. This in turn leads to health problems and instability.

• Rounded corners and soft curves help the energy flow, whereas sharp corners and angled shapes disrupt the natural rhythms.

shades of white

fresh
spiritual
brilliant
bright
dazzling
pure
peaceful
clean
elegant
new
calming
serene
understated
perfect
energizing

Our journey begins in a neutral state with shades of white. Here the colours white and cream and stone combine with natural elements to give a style that has an almost universal and timeless appeal. It is the closest to modernity that we get.

It is no surprise then, that despite offering some forty colours in our paint range, stone and white are by far the biggest selling colours; they are definitely the most popular choice for our painted furniture too. Little wonder when you consider that a dresser or armoire painted white would look good in whatever room or circumstances it found itself.

But be warned. There is more to shades of white than just a simple can of magnolia - and the key word here is 'tones'. White is a colour, too, and just like all the rest it can take a great deal of searching to find the appropriate shade. Sometimes, only a brilliant white will do, but it can look cold and harsh. A knocked-back antique white is more palatable, but it can adopt a grey or greenish tinge in some lights. White on white, however, always works.

White and its close relatives are a perfect backdrop for an eclectic style, whether you are into urban-modern with fake-fur trimmings, or rustic-country with a passion for antique-oddities. As a family of colours, whites and their related shades have the ability to cross boundaries of any decorating style. Who can dispute the universal appeal of such delicious combinations as sparkling white china, linen and lace, or the glamour of white feathers against a textured cotton?

Shades of white is also about texture. Those stunning white houses in Greece or Spain that we all admire and covet are as much about the texture of the rough plaster as they are about the light and brightness of the white. Nature and wood are easy partners, as are wool, wire, stone, pebbles, chalk and driftwood. They each work together in harmony. Natural fibres and fabrics look fresh and invigorating, black and white photographs distinguished and sane. Given its ageless qualities, white allows you to successfully combine modern materials like concrete and steel with a white backdrop.

elements of the style

Witty and sensual: a feather boa sewn to a linen lampshade. For a touch of modernity, glavanized tin platters and trays.

For windows, use simple poles and plain white muslin or cotton tied with bows. Here's Emerald, making a timely appearance.

projects

On an eminently practical note, our projects for this chapter begin with a faux stone floor, completely fake, of course, but possessing all the qualities of the real thing and more (pages 40-3). It is the starting point for a whole cornucopia of flooring ideas featured throughout the book. We look at texture with a three-dimensional pattern created with only filler and card (pages 44-5), and extol the virtues once again of printing ink-based fabric paints: this time with a somewhat surprisingly white-on-white print that features the help of a most unexpected computer mouse-pad (pages 48-9)! And finally, proving that we do occasionally flirt with modernity, brilliant shiny instant finials (pages 50-1) are followed by a handsome cement candle holder (pages 52-3).

faux stone floor

Of all the techniques or concepts that we've ever created, it seems that the faux stone floor, or faux tiling, has provoked the greatest reaction and fascination - probably due to its simplicity and huge application. After all, a tiled floor is highly covetable and normally very expensive, too. A tiled floor this may be, but although on first acquaintance it resembles stone, it is, in fact, made entirely from medium density fibreboard (MDF). This material is extraordinarily versatile and economic to use and furthermore, it is wonderfully warm underfoot (unlike the real thing).

To achieve the stone appearance of the floor you will need to use a colourwash technique - it's just diluted paint with water that is spread across the surface with a cloth (otherwise known as 'ragging-in') to create a haphazard transparent wash - which makes each tile unique and adding authenticity. Best of all, it is virtually foolproof when used on such small pieces. For a warmer feel, take a look at the Pebble Border floor on pages 134-5, which is even easier to recreate as the tiles were literally just painted with our own terracotta-coloured paint - the realism is quite astounding.

The other important factor is the use of acrylic floor varnish - certainly one of the best inventions of the decade. It is hard-wearing and easy-to-use, there are no powerful fumes and it has an initial drying time of just a few minutes.

If you don't own a jigsaw, don't panic, because there is one last nugget to impart: most hardware stores will now pre-cut timber for you, leaving only the infills to tackle. So to make your own fine faux floor, all you need is a cutting plan, some painting skills and a good pair of knees (sorry, we can't take that part away!).

MATERIALS

9mm ($^3/_8$in) plywood sheets
12mm ($^1/_2$in) MDF cut to required size for tiles and border
Thick 'block-out' vinyl emulsion (latex) paint in White
10cm (4in) paintbrush
Water-based paint in Antique White and Mustard Yellow
Water-based colourwash in Stone, mixed 1 part paint to 8 parts water
Bristle paintbrush
Soft cloth
Acrylic floor varnish
Paint kettle
Flat plate
5cm (2in) roller
Rubber stamp
Tile adhesive with flexible additive
Waterproof grout
Trowel or squeegee

Creating the faux stone floor

To recreate this stunning faux stone floor you first need to design a floorplan so that you can assess whether you need half-tiles and infills in your design. It is useful to know this prior to cutting the timber. For added authenticity, round off the edges on each tile with sandpaper before painting and, as ever, when cutting or sanding MDF, wear a protective mask against the dust. If the surface you wish to tile is slightly uneven, line your floor with 9mm (³/₈in) plywood held in position with screws.

When painting and varnishing the tiles, do ensure you pay particular attention to the sides, to prevent any moisture damage from the grout. Then, for the adhesive and grouting, always use professional quality tiling adhesive and grout (with an additive to make them flexible and provide extra adhesion to the wood) in powder form. These products are available from tile merchants and full instructions are provided on the packs. There are two varieties, one a quick-setting version, where each mix is workable for about 35 minutes, or a much slower one which takes 24 hours to cure. Never use the ready-mixed varieties nor the combined adhesive and grout – they are not used by professional tilers and they seem to contain ingredients that actually harm the acrylic varnish and can cause damage to your painted tiles.

1 Preparing the MDF tiles

Prime the tiles with a base coat of the white vinyl emulsion (latex), taking care to include the sides. Allow to dry thoroughly and then paint with a coat of Antique White.

2 Applying the colourwash

Brush on the Stone colourwash and 'rag-in' with a soft cloth, leaving a thin trace of colour. If necessary, repeat with a stronger solution. Apply two coats of floor varnish, especially on the sides.

3 Creating a border

Paint Mustard Yellow on the edges of the border tiles. Load the roller with paint from the plate and apply to the stamp. Press down firmly and repeat. Leave to dry and varnish.

4 Fixing the tiles

Working a small area at a time, use tile adhesive to secure your tiles to the floor – leaving a small gap between each tile for the grout. Allow to dry for 24 hours.

5 Grouting the tiles

Your tiles are now ready for grouting with a small trowel or squeegee. Work over a small area of the floor at a time and then polish off any excess grout with a soft damp cloth.

6 The finishing touch

Apply one or two more coats of acrylic floor varnish as a finishing touch – this will help to keep your grout clean and white and your floor looking pristine.

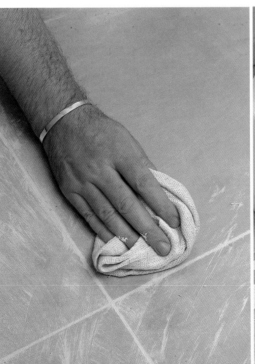

plaster wall relief

The papier-mâché frieze in our last book was, without a doubt, one of the most successful projects. Here's an even simpler way to provide texture or a three-dimensional pattern to liven up a plain wall. Here we have created a pattern all over the wall featuring several motifs and, by using filler, have given the finished effect a powdery quality. The idea works especially well as a border at dado height or just above the skirting board, or indeed around a door or window.

To create an accurate and regular repeat you need to create a square template, the width of which equals the distance between each element of the required pattern. If you do not have sticky-backed plastic, you could use a plastic folder kept in place with a spray adhesive.

MATERIALS
Spirit level
Plank of wood
Pen or pencil
Square template
Art or mounting board
Sticky-backed plastic or plastic folder and spray adhesive
Scalpel
Masking tape
Tub ready-mixed filler
Palette knife

1 Creating the pattern
Draw a vertical line on the wall using a spirit level and wooden plank. Then mark the motif positions using the square template. Draw a horizontal line at each mark.

2 Cutting the template
Cut the art or mounting board into a small square and draw your design onto it. Then cover the design with the sticky-backed plastic and carefully cut around the outline with the scalpel.

3 Applying the filler
Tape the template at each mark and fill with the filler using the palette knife. Scrape off the excess as you work. Immediately remove the template each time the motif is finished.

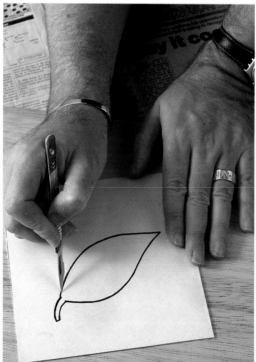
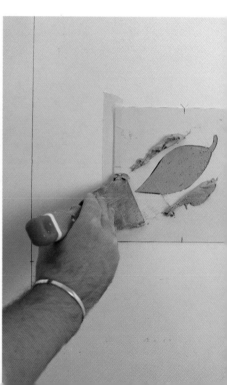

printed curtains

Block printing is the perfect way to create a professional-looking repeat. We chose a Matisse-like design and used a computer mouse-pad to create the stamp (well, someone had to...). Rubber-sheeting would be fine.

The vital ingredient, though, is the fabric paint – the ones that are based on printing-inks are the best as, thanks to the base medium, a little paint goes a long way without much loss of tone. To create this oyster white, diluted Yellow and Black were added in minute quantities to the White (for mixing, see page 137) – make sure you mix enough to tackle the whole project as matching dyes later would be almost impossible (300ml [½ pint] base medium is enough for approximately 3m [3yd] of fabric).

MATERIALS

Mouse pad

Spray adhesive

Scalpel

2 blocks of wood

All-purpose glue

White ticking or similar

Drapers' chalk

Fabric paint base medium

Fabric paints in White, Yellow and Black

5cm (2in) roller and plate

Eyelet kit

1 Cutting the stamp
Photocopy your design to size, stick it to the shiny side of the mouse pad with spray adhesive and cut out the centre of the design with the scalpel. Glue each piece to one of the wooden blocks.

2 Creating the pattern
Measure and mark guide lines for the stamps using drapers' chalk. Then stamp alternate squares with the reversed-out design applying the fabric paint to the stamp with the roller. Then fill all the remaining gaps with the other stamp.

3 Fixing the eyelets
Press a 5cm (2in) hem at the top of each curtain and mark and punch out eyelet holes with the cutter at regular intervals (see manufacturer's instructions). Fix the eyelets with the gun and thread on rope or string.

curtain pole & finials

It is said that the simplest design ideas are often the most successful and that is something we certainly subscribe to. That statement would definitely apply to our curtain pole and finials. Inspired on a shoot for television by what appeared to be plastic lemons fixed to a pole (and why not?), we gave the concept a little more elegance by using these metal bottle stoppers as finials. Nowadays, bottle stoppers come in all shapes and sizes, in metal, glass or plastic and, as you can plainly see, they make just perfect finials for a wooden curtain pole. Here is style and elegance and, what is more, with the simple fixing method, you can change them easily and cheaply whenever the mood takes you.

MATERIALS
26mm (1in) diameter dowel rod
Water-based woodstain in Dark Brown
5cm (2in) paintbrush
Acrylic dead-flat (satin) varnish
Drill with 16mm ($^5/_8$in) and 6mm ($^1/_4$in) drill bits
2 bottle stoppers
Rawlplugs
60mm (2$^1/_4$in) screws

1 Staining the pole
Cut the dowel rod to the correct size and then stain it all over with the water-based woodstain. When dry, seal the pole with one or two coats of acrylic dead-flat (satin) varnish to protect the stain.

2 Fixing the finials
Using a workbench or vice for support, carefully drill a 16mm ($^5/_8$in) hole at each end of the pole. Then simply insert the cork end of each stopper into the holes until the stoppers lie neatly flush with the ends.

3 Fixing the pole
Using the 6mm ($^1/_4$in) drill bit, drill a hole through the pole approximately 5cm (2in) from each end and at the corresponding position on the wall. Use rawlplugs and long screws to fix to the wall.

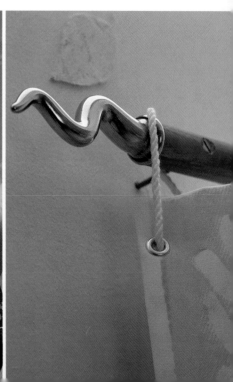

cement candle holder

A never-ceasing passion for candles and the ease with which ready-mixed cement can be used were the inspiration behind this project. To use the cement, just make a mould or use a container, mix the cement with water and pour in. Use cement rather than concrete, as it is smoother and a lighter grey when dry.

When filling the mould, always leave a small gap at the top to allow for expansion when inserting the night-light (candle) containers. For added strength, we placed long pieces of florist wire in a criss-cross pattern in the base of the mould in a small amount of the cement before adding the balance. Also consider lining the base with felt to prevent scratching.

MATERIALS
Cement mix
Water
Mixing bucket
Trowel
MDF or plywood board
5 x 2.5cm (2 x 1in) timber battens
Panel pins (brads)
Night-lights (candles)
Water-based paint in Antique White (optional)

1 Mixing the cement
Just before it is needed, mix the cement in a large plastic bucket following the manufacturer's guidelines. Ensure that all the dry powder is absorbed into the water before moving to the next step.

2 Creating a mould
Using the board as a base, fix the battens in place with the panel pins (brads) to create a mould. Carefully pour the mixed cement into the mould, level off and sink the night-light (candle) cases in place as shown.

3 Finishing touches
When the cement is completely dry (see manufacturer's instructions), remove the battens. The concrete looks fine on its own, but painted with a water-based paint (say, in Antique White) is effective too.

mediterranean shades

passion

sunflowers

islands

lavender

fruits

golden

balmy

warmth

sunlit

poppy

white

orange-grove

fruits

glowing

azure

The Mediterranean is all about passion - a passion for life, for strong colour and for relaxed living. It is a region steeped in traditions, using local materials to perfection and where nature is a *tour de force* when it comes to an inspirational palette. More than any other style, though, it is about a bold simplicity and minimalism of a natural scale. As such, it is in tune with current trends.

The areas surrounding the Mediterranean have always been a great centre for trading and commerce and were the heart of Western culture for centuries - this mix is reflected in modern day Mediterranean style. From a colour perspective, the palette is as rich and varied as the natural world that inspires it: the blues and whites of Greece, the aquamarines, blues, reds and greens of Provence, the ice-cream pastels of Italian frescos, and the earthy reds and ochres of North Africa. We deal with the latter in our Shades of Spice chapter.

These bold colours can be timeless. Certainly blue and white have been used for centuries and are every bit as invigorating now as then - and blues travel well into more Northern shores. Care has to be taken when trying to recreate the bright primaries, though. Without the sun-drenched backdrop of the Mediterranean they can look harsh and tainted; they need to be bleached by white light for perfection.

This said, to emulate the warmth of this area is no lofty ideal. It is attainable and effective, and by meticulously blurring the boundaries between outdoor life and indoor living, a seamless transfer can be successfully achieved, evoking that feel-good factor we crave. Consider using rugs and runners made of sisal or rush casually laid around the home rather than fitted carpets made of wool; and incorporate furnishings made of wicker, canvas or metal. For window treatments, use blinds, sheers or shutters, and for walls nothing more than paint will do. If you are a cautious decorator, use cool, pale shades as your backdrop and paint the furniture in more vibrant tones - a great way to transform even the humblest piece. If you hanker after a less contrived, less decorated look, then this is the area for you.

elements of the style

Fill with olives,
fruit and vegetables
like artichokes or
peppers, and
succulent plants.

Seek out old wire trays and kitchen
utensils and mix with chunky
ceramics and earthenware jugs.

Drink wine from
bistro-style
glasses and, for
a touch of
luxury, use soaps
in bright warm
colours. A bottle
of linen water to
hand brightens up
washday chores.

Eau de linge
à la lavande
pour le fer a repasser
linen lavender water

projects

Paint is still the most popular finish in the Mediterranean and as you will see in this chapter, modern-day colourwashing can emulate the chalky limewash or distempers of the past, while hiding the imperfections of a wall. Colourwashing works brilliantly on our MDF tiles, too, as seen on a second visit to the faux tiled floor (pages 70-1). We also look at just how successful a contrasting or complementary faded border can be when rubbed-back or sponged to simulate years of age (pages 78-9). For our window treatment, we have thrown caution to the wind by creating some simple wooden shutters so sublime we'd swear you would never guess their origin (pages 74-7). Finally, and these projects are simplicity itself, we show you how to make a wooden shelf (pages 68-9) and some brightly painted tablelinen (pages 80-1).

rustic wire shelf

The wavy edge to this shelf is reminiscent of Mediterranean country style used a lot in simple Greek and French furniture. Thankfully, mouldings like this are inexpensive and readily available at timber merchants or hardware stores. And although most of the designs are not in the slightest way suitable for shelving like this, the one used here is just perfect. The drabness of the stone-coloured paint with which it has been painted is a useful counterpoint to calm the heat and brightness of the blues surrounding it and is a surprisingly wonderful colour for displaying 'objets'.

When planning your shelf, make sure that you cut it to a length where the ends, plus the side-panels, finish with a complete wave. It is worth being meticulous so that the overall design looks balanced.

MATERIALS
Wooden shelf panel 18mm ($^5/_8$in) thick, cut to size
Decorative moulding, cut to size (1 front and 2 sides)
12 x 12mm ($^1/_2$ x $^1/_2$in) batten for rear of shelf, cut to size
25mm (1in) panel pins (brads)
Water-based paints in Stone and Moroccan Earth
Acrylic dead-flat (satin) varnish
Wire gauge 1.6mm ($^1/_{16}$in)
2 dowel rods
Wire gauge 0.9mm ($^1/_{32}$in)

1 Fixing moulding to shelf
Pin the mouldings so the front panel overlaps and hides the side ones. Fix the batten to the rear underside. Paint with Stone paint and varnish.

2 Twisting the wire
Wrap the ends of the thicker wire around one dowel rod, loop the other end to the second rod. Stand on the first rod and turn the other until the wire is twisted enough.

3 Making the brackets
Fold the twisted wire into a bracket shape and join the ends together. Cover by coiling on the thinner wire. Paint with Moroccan Earth and varnish.

checked tiled floor

We confess: the floor used for this set had a former life in the previous chapter (see pages 40-3), ably proving just how versatile the MDF floor tile concept is. For a completely different look we removed some of the original grout, re-painted the 'tiles' and then varnished and re-grouted: transformed without the need for laying new tiles. The whole floor was then varnished one more time to help keep the grout good and clean.

We also added half-tiles to make a decorative border which extends the impact of the floor and solves the problem of having to instal skirting. However, the main success of this particular floor is due to the colourwash, the translucent hue of the blue is exactly like that of a ceramic tile, positively Etruscan, and it is remarkably easy to achieve.

MATERIALS

Vinyl matt emulsion (latex) in Blue

2 Cornflower Blue colourwashes: 1 part paint to 10 parts water; and 1 part paint to 8 parts water

Soft cloth

Water-based paint in Antique White

Stone colourwash: 1 part paint to 10 parts water

Medium grade sandpaper

Artists' fixative

Satin acrylic floor varnish

---

1 Painting the tiles
Paint two coats of emulsion (latex) on half the tiles (sides, too). Brush on weaker wash and 'rag-in' with cloth. Repeat with stronger mix.

2 Sanding-back the edges
Repeat on the remaining tiles with the Antique White paint and Stone wash. Sand back the edges of all the tiles for a less pristine – and more authentic – look.

3 Applying the varnish
Spray the tiles with artists' fixative to prevent the wash from moving and when dry apply two coats of the floor varnish, covering the edges as well.

Tile variations

To recreate Italian blue and white 'flag' tiles (left), Antique White is the base aged with a wash of Stone. The patterns are painted in Cornflower Blue, with a wash of Providence Blue. The brightly coloured tiles (below left) have white added to each colour for the base coat subsequently washed over with a diluted version. For the patterns, Antique White has been decorated in the same way. All were rubbed back with wire wool. The floor to the right has been painted Terracotta and the insets washed in Cornflower Blue. The star design has been stamped on.

distressed shutters

Wooden shutters are to be found on most buildings in the Mediterranean - on anything from magnificent chateaux to elegant villas, or on the more humble village or town houses and they serve two purposes. One, they provide shade, shelter and privacy from the burning sun, and two, they offer added security if the house is left uninhabited for long periods or if, due to the heat, the windows need to be open all of the time. For this last reason, shutters are often slatted to allow a free flow of air although for larger windows and doors, a more solid timber version is generally used.

To a degree, the same note of caution concerning the use of bright Mediterranean colours expressed earlier applies when considering the use of shutters. Commonplace they may be in sunnier climes, they could look a little redundant when battling against more Northern grey and heavy skies. Nevertheless, they do suit this particular style of decorating, especially in a bathroom or kitchen, and with such rustic style can be used to great effect. Fixed to the window frame, they adapt quite easily to internal use; lying flat against the wall when maximum light is required and giving extra warmth and security when closed, they are a surprisingly practical and attractive alternative to curtains.

Few would think that the shutters shown here were bulk-standard new timber panels acquired from any local hardware store - even the rusty brackets look ancient. The secret lies in the ageing and painting. For a more natural scheme, you could consider liming the shutters instead of the distressed paint effect given overleaf.

MATERIALS

Sufficient lengths of planed pine to construct two shutters, cut to fit window or recess, minimum thickness 12mm ($\frac{1}{2}$in)

12 lengths of the same timber cut to the width of each shutter as horizontal battens

Blowtorch

Wire brush

Liming paste

5cm (2in) paintbrush

Medium grade wire wool

Acrylic dead-flat (satin) varnish

Panel pins (brads)

Hammer

Latex-based adhesive

Water-based paints in Apple Green, Caspian Blue (slightly diluted with water) and Moroccan Earth

Wire-wool or sandpaper

4 gate hinges plus fixing screws

Spray paint in Silver

2 lengths of 48 x 20mm (2 x $\frac{3}{4}$in) batten for the side panels

Making the shutters

Shutters are a practical and highly decorative window dressing. By being an effective draught excluder and provider of extra security, they beat the ubiquitous roller blind by a mile. Furthermore, they are relatively easy to make, especially if you ask the hardware store to pre-cut the timber for you. Indeed, if the window does not permit an exact number of planks across the width, consider adding a thin strip of timber that can be used to camouflage the gap, rather than any tricky manoeuvres with a saw.

If you wish to avoid the process of raising the grain, but still want a vaguely rustic appearance, use sawn timber which has a more determined, rougher grain and age it with the help of a diluted grey woodstain - this would eliminate steps 1 and 2 below. The ageing technique for the gate hinges is the same as for the Simple Curtain Pole, as shown on pages 100-1. For added security, you could add a catch or wooden bar across the panels - although few potential intruders would continue the invasion when faced with your shutters.

1 Raising the grain
Use the blowtorch to scorch the surface of the wood, moving the torch slowly along the grain. Repeat on both sides and then clean out the charred wood with the wire brush, again following the direction of the grain. Wipe both sides of the wood with a damp cloth.

2 Liming the wood
Paint on the liming paste evenly both along the grain and across the grain. Let the liming paste dry, and then burnish it off with wire wool leaving as little of the surface liming paste as possible. To seal the remains of the paste, apply one coat of the acrylic dead-flat (satin) varnish.

3 Constructing the shutters
Lay a sufficient number of the vertical planks for one shutter on a table or bench. Then secure the double-rows of horizontal battens with panel pins (brads) at the top, middle and bottom. Carefully turn over the shutter and pin it from the front too.

4 **Applying the resist**
Use the latex-based adhesive as a resist on the shutters and side panels. Paint it on in haphazard patches concentrating on the edges, sides and top. Allow to dry and paint on one coat of Apple Green, leave to dry, and then apply the diluted Caspian Blue.

5 **Sanding-back**
Use wire-wool or sandpaper to gently sand-back the paint – the glue will come off in haphazard welts, revealing the limed wood below. Reminiscent of aged and peeling paint, the Apple Green will also show through the diluted Caspian Blue top coat without too much effort.

6 **Fixing the brackets**
Paint, age and varnish the gate hinges as described on page 100 and fix to the shutter as shown below with screws, making sure there is a horizontal batten beneath. Finally, secure the side-battens to the window frame and fix the shutters to them by the hinges.

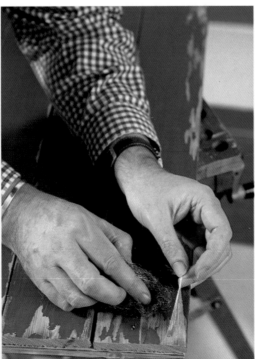

colourwashed wall

Over the years we have seen many an authoritative guide as to how to create a colourwash, but unless you really want that particular radical Andy Warhol/New York Loft look, most are to be avoided. There is no doubt that the most successful washes are the ones based on building up 'tones' - whether you apply ten layers or two, as in our method, where we eliminate several layers by starting with a pastel base.

Most people find that once 'washed', flat colour painting becomes a thing of the past. Getting the correct consistency for a wash can be tricky - it is always better to over-dilute rather than under-dilute a wash and then apply an extra layer if you think it is necessary. Also, always make sufficient wash to complete the whole room as matching a wash is virtually impossible.

Faded borders are very common on the exterior of whitewashed Mediterranean houses, but once again they lose something in the translation to cooler, greyer light. However, used internally they are a tremendous way of making a feature of a window and when used as a border, are a perfect partner to a colourwash.

1 **Applying the colourwash**
Paint on a flat coat of matt emulsion (latex) and let dry. With broad strokes, paint on the weaker wash in a small area and 'rag-in'. Complete the wall and repeat with stronger wash.

2 **Masking the border**
Mark out the required border with drapers' chalk and use this as a guide for positioning the masking tape. Use the straight-edge or spirit level as necessary to make sure it is true.

3 **Sponging on the paint**
Put a little of the mixed blue paint in the tray and use the sponge to apply it, dabbing off any excess paint on newspaper first. Leave some areas more exposed than others.

MATERIALS

Vinyl matt emulsion
(latex) in Pale Blue
Paintbrush
2 Provence Blue
colourwashes: one, mixed
1 part paint to 8 parts
water; the other, 1 part
paint to 6 parts water
Soft cloth
Drapers' chalk
Masking tape
Straight-edge or spirit
level
Water-based paints in
Gustavian Blue and
Cornflower, mixed in
equal quantities
Plate or tray
Natural sponge

painted tablelinen

Here is a simple, contemporary design for a set of Mediterranean-style tablecloth and napkins reminiscent of Italy or Greece, that is ludicrously easy to achieve. The secret is to use the printing ink-based fabric paints used on the Printed Curtains in the previous chapter (see pages 48-9) as a little goes a long way. This is achieved by the base medium extender and the fact that the paint is diluted with water. Here, ticking has been used, but any cotton or bleached calico would do.

When using fabric paints, always put plastic sheeting beneath the fabric to prevent the paints staining your worksurface. The darker colours in particular can be very difficult to remove.

MATERIALS

White ticking, cut to size

Fabric paints in Ultramarine, Purple and Black

Fabric paint base medium

Paint kettle

Water

Drapers' chalk

Ruler

Paintbrush

Plastic sheet

Small paint roller (optional)

Scalpel (optional)

1 Mixing the paint
Add the Ultramarine paint to the base medium and mix. Add the diluted Purple and Black, drop by drop to the desired shade (see also page 137). Thin with water to the consistency of single cream.

2 Painting the border
Mark a guideline on the fabric with the drapers' chalk. Paint on the fabric paint (don't forget the plastic sheeting) and when dry, repeat on the reverse side. Fix with an iron as described in the manufacturer's instructions.

3 Creating other patterns
Softer, more haphazard stripes can be created using a mini-paint roller. Carefully cut to size using a scalpel and use a plate or tray to hold the paint so that you can push the roller through the paint to load it.

scandinavian colours

candles

driftwood

fjords

solace

bleached

lakes

modern

berry-red

distemper

cotton

simplicity

wholesome

damask

checks

stripes

It's funny, but we have never particularly associated ourselves with Scandinavian or Swedish style. But there are some remarkable similarities - where Grand meets humble, possibly. On the one hand, never has there been a decorating style more dedicated to paint. It is used everywhere from ceilings to floors, on walls, panelling, windows and accessories; and painted borders are a particular trademark. Furthermore, Scandinavian paint is a beautiful paint: a chalky limewash that fades with age, not dissimilar to our own version of acrylic distemper. Even more to the point, it is also the style known to take the best from something and then pare it down to the significant essentials - another Grand Illusions speciality.

For the purposes of this chapter, we have put aside the modern achievements of the region (without diminishing them), to concentrate instead on their traditional past. The Scandinavian influence has travelled far, to the USA and to Eastern Europe and Germany, and has travelled well with time too.

The classic lines and subtle tones of Gustavian style have just as much a place today as they did in the past. Swedish colours, the glowing ochres, the diluted blues, the muted reds, as well as the creams and whites, work well with natural materials like stone and wood. The use of symmetry and placement brings tranquillity and calm to a room.

For a region that spends so much of its time in darkness, it is not surprising that the Scandinavians are masters of preserving and enhancing light, both with pale colours on walls and floors and with the skilful use of glass, mirrors, muslins and candles. The end result is a beautiful, harmonious, rustic elegance, borne out of poverty rather than any aesthetic crusade.

It is for the Scandinavian beliefs in reducing rather than adding, rejuvenating rather than replacing, and for the way they bring value to possessions that a place has been found in *New Decorating*. Their style is both unassuming and unpretentious and, as such, is accessible to even the most timid of decorators.

elements of the style

The Scandinavians combine old and new with great success. This handsome antique coffee pot sits comfortably next to our fake crystal candlesticks.

Pale soft rugs, simple checked cottons and ribbons mix together effortlessly for a classic but timeless look.

These witty ceramics by
contemporary potter
Judith Rowe have great
charm. And rough meets
smooth with some chunky
concrete pots nesting in
an old iron planter.

Duck Egg Blue on Vanilla

Elephant Grey on Antique White

Stockholm Blue on Antique White　　　Antique Lime on Antique White

Buttermilk and Olive Green

Barley and Gustavian Blue

Adobe Red and Elephant Grey

Stone and New England Red

Adobe Red and Elephant Grey

projects

The projects for this chapter concentrate on the simplicity of Scandinavian style, where a little speaks a lot. We start with an instant curtain pole and extol the virtues of modern-day curtain clips, aged to look like period pieces (pages 100-1). Our passion for sconces is then revealed with two variations on the theme, again a starting point for a whole gamut of ideas using thin brass pipe (pages 102-5). Then we finish with aged and painted walls and floors (pages 106-9) making great play of a Gustavian-style border and incorporating a shelf edged with decorative moulding.

simple curtain pole

As you can probably guess, one of our greatest decorating passions is slightly rusty, simple curtain poles; slightly rusty anything, come to that. Having already discovered that our Moroccan Earth paint gives a distinctly pleasing aged appearance, we have now found the delights of an ageing fluid.

Available in two types, cold patinating fluid will age brass and copper to a mid-brown or an almost-black finish in next-to-no-time. Be warned though, it is extremely caustic and should be handled with care – also, many modern brass products have a protective lacquer on them which needs to be removed first; full instructions are on the pack: read them carefully!

MATERIALS

8mm (³/₈in) diameter dowel rod
Water-based paint in Moroccan Earth
Spray paint in Silver
Acrylic dead-flat (satin) varnish
Brass curtain clips
Cold patinating fluid
Old narrow paint brush
Jade oil
Right-angled brass hooks
Bradawl (awl)

1 Preparing the pole
Cut the pole to size and paint with two coats of the Moroccan Earth water-based paint. When dry, spray a light mist of silver paint. Finish with two coats of dead-flat (satin) varnish.

2 Ageing the curtain clips
Dilute the cold patinating fluid with water and brush it onto the clips until they are completely blackened. Do this over a bowl to catch any excess. Allow the fluid to dry, finish with jade oil and then leave for 24 hours.

3 Fixing the pole
Drill and plug the wall if necessary and screw in the right-angled brass hooks. Make small holes in the pole with the bradawl (awl) in corresponding positions and gently press the pole onto the hooks.

skinny sconces

Since experimenting with tin in the last book, we've been searching for a way to create a candleholder without the need of some serious metalworking. Thankfully, a local plumbing department provided the necessary key and the same technique was used to create the Wooden Mirror Sconces overleaf.

Aside from the thin brass tubing, the critical ingredient here is the zinc threaded rod, as it stops the brass tube from buckling when you bend it. The other major find was the pipe reducer, normally used where thick pipe meets thin. It just happens to look like a delicate candle-cup and with a bit of help, fits snugly over the brass tubing. If you need a larger candle-cup, see the next project, overleaf.

MATERIALS

Brass pipe 6mm (¼in) diameter
Zinc steel threaded rod 4mm (⅛in) diameter
Hack saw
Hammer
Drill with 3mm (⅛in) bit
Fabric tape or string
Brass pipe reducer
All-purpose glue
Water-based paint in Moroccan Earth or
Cold patinating fluid and jade oil

1 Cutting the pipe

Cut the brass pipe to length and then the zinc thread 5cm (2in) shorter. Insert the thread into the pipe so that it is flush at one end of the pipe.

2 Bending the pipe

Holding the pipe firmly at each end, use a table leg to carefully bend it into a curve. Then flatten the top of the sconce with a hammer and drill two small holes for fixing it to the wall.

3 Creating the candle cup

Wrap tape or string around the tip of the sconce to ensure a snug fit into the pipe reducer and glue in place. Paint with Moroccan Earth or age with cold patinating fluid and jade oil.

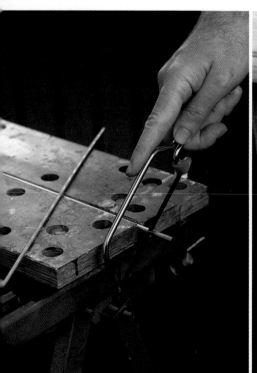

wooden mirror sconces

To provide light from the walls in addition to the ceiling, the Scandinavians used wall sconces and the beauty of the mirrored sconce was that, like a crystal chandelier, it magnified the light. Bevelled edges, etching and gilding were all used as devices to create more surfaces for the light to bounce off. Here, we've taken the technique of the Skinny Sconces on the previous page and added it to a mirrored backing. The zinc thread provides another useful service, this time acting as the fixing for both the candle-cup and for fitting the sconce to the wood.

You can age the brass tubing with the cold patinating fluid, as before, or indeed paint with Moroccan Earth paint if you prefer. Ageing the mirror with paint stripper complements the overall appearance.

Using the 16mm (⁵⁄₈in) diameter brass rod (the pipe normally used for hanging rails in wardrobes) will allow you to use thicker candles. Instead of using the dowel rod to keep the candle cap in place, you could use a simple cork, cut to size.

1 **Creating the back plate**
Cut the corners off the back and round-off with sandpaper – also sand-off any rough edges on the mini-battens. Paint with New England Red, and then the back with Admiral Blue and battens with Mustard. Varnish.

2 **Ageing the mirror**
Dab random amounts of the paint stripper onto the back of the mirror to simulate ageing. Wait for 20 minutes and rub-back with wire wool. Secure to the wooden back with the adhesive pads and carefully pin the battens in place.

3 **Creating the sconce**
Cut and insert the zinc thread into the pipe so that 15mm (⁵⁄₈in) protrudes at each end. Bend it into shape. Drill a hole in the dowel and sconce and join together – push the candle cap onto the dowel and glue.

MATERIALS

Piece of wood 380 x 130 x
15mm (15 x 5 x ⅝in)

Hack saw

Medium grade sandpaper

2 battens, each 100 x 15
x 8mm (4 x ⅝ x ⅜in)

Water-based paint in New
England Red, Admiral Blue
(a mix of Cornflower and
Gustavian Blue) and
Mustard

Acrylic dead-flat (satin)
varnish

Mirror or mirror tile
approximately 300 x 100mm
(12 x 4in)

Paint stripper

Medium grade wire wool

Adhesive pads

Panel pins (brads)

Hammer

Zinc steel threaded rod
4mm (⅛in) diameter

Brass rod 6mm (¼in)
diameter

Drill with 6mm (¼in) bit

10-15mm (⅜-⅝in) dowel

rod 15mm (⅝in) diameter

25mm (1in) brass rod 16mm
(⅝in) diameter

All-purpose glue

aged wooden shelf

Tongue-and-groove deserves to be immortalized as one of the greatest design classics of our time, for while being a brilliant means with which to conceal a problem or hitherto boring wall, it also provides warmth and enormous character to a room. Now, we're not talking the stained and lacquered variety here, as displayed so eminently by most hardware stores, we're talking romantic, painted and gently aged if you please. By using paints like ours, you will be authentically recreating the soft and chalky distempered look that the Scandinavians loved.

The type of wood used here is quite formal. For a looser look, use planks of rough sawn timber: it has a more textured appearance and when varying widths are used, looks like it has been on the walls for decades.

MATERIALS
Tongue-and-groove panels fixed to the walls with battens, 20mm (³/₄in) panel pins (brads) and wall hammer bolts
Water-based paint in New England Red, Stockholm Blue and Stone
Medium grade sandpaper
Timber for shelf and supports
Mitre saw
Acrylic dead-flat (satin) varnish
Drill with 3mm (¹/₈in) bit
Countersink tool and filler

1 **Ageing the wood panelling** Paint two coats of New England Red and one or two of Stockholm Blue onto the panelling. Distress the edges by rubbing-back with sandpaper.

2 **Cutting the shelf supports** Use the mitre saw to cut the timber at 45° to make the shelf supports. Paint and age these, with the shelf, as in Step 1, and apply two coats of varnish.

3 **Fixing the brackets and shelf** Position the shelf and, using a spirit level, drill and screw the supports. Countersink, fill and paint (New England Red and then Stone) as required.

aged floor & skirting

The humble painted floor seems to capture everyone's imagination, yet fills a person with unnecessary fear at the same time. But abandon those thoughts, this really is one of the easiest ways to solve your flooring problems, and something that the Scandinavians excelled at.

For our room, we simply painted the floor with diluted white household glue (full instructions are on the pack) and then two coats of Gustavian Blue, followed by three coats of acrylic floor varnish, allowing each one to dry thoroughly before starting the next.

Painted borders also add scale to a room and were used to divide sections or create panels or frames. Our faded stripe on the skirting gives a point of interest to what is, after all, a very tonal scheme.

MATERIALS

White household glue
Water-based paints in
Gustavian Blue, New England
Red, Stone and Providence Blue
Acrylic floor varnish
Latex-based household glue or
masking fluid
Medium grade sandpaper
Masking tape
Soft stencil brush
Medium grade wire wool
Acrylic dead-flat (satin)
varnish

1 Preparing
Paint the skirting with two coats of New England Red. When dry, apply glue in random patches where ageing is to be simulated. When dry apply two coats of Stone.

2 Sanding back the top coat
Use sandpaper to rub gently all along the skirting first and then concentrate on the ageing areas – where you applied the glue. This will begin to peel off in patches as you sand. Remove the rest by hand.

3 Creating and ageing a border
Use masking tape to create a border and stipple Providence Blue randomly with the stencil brush. Allow some of the base to show. Rub back more with wire wool, remove tape, and varnish.

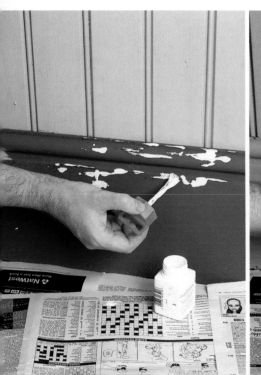

shades of spice

mosaic

adobe

jewel

paprika

seed

temple

peaceful

cinnamon

baked

saffron

terracotta

warmth

shrine

cardamom

aromatic

In our interpretation, Shades of Spice has no real geographic or political borders. Rather, the rich, dark, earthy colours could easily be indigenous to the East, North Africa, Mexico or India, but they are united by a global spirit. Decorating in this style is, once again, an uncluttered business, built on a territory steeped with history and skilled local crafts. Local materials have been used to perfection, with Mother Nature keeping a watchful eye. In France, due to historic events, the North Africa influence is especially strong and, given its location, it is hardly surprising that there is much crossover between this and Mediterranean influences.

Here is another land blasted by the sun, and cool shady interiors are high on the list of priorities. Windows and doorways tend to be small and the light and heat is often diffused with a wrought-iron grill or shutters where religion dictates a secluded and secular lifestyle. To more Western eyes, the screens and grills have great value for their decorative and evocative designs.

Intricate patterns are also evident in superb mosaics and tiles. There is great similarity between the ornate patterns from, say, Morocco, which often incorporate Islamic symbols and those of, say, Mexico or South America. In these countries, ceramic tiles and marble or stone floors are frequently used for their innate coolness, and textiles are rich in decoration and often brightened by gold or sequins. All of these finishes are designed to provide a rich but safe haven away from the heat and dust outside.

But it is the richness of colour that really has the greatest appeal in Shades of Spice - the almost-dirty, muddy tones that provide a subtle warmth: yellow ochre, adobe red, and earthy brown combined with natural tones of terracotta or stone. Once again, there is an element of bringing outdoor life into the interior. For a distinctly colonial air, mix rattan and bamboo with wrought-iron furniture; use tiles, ceramics and plenty of greenery for decoration; and for rich tones, add a touch of gold or silver.

elements of the style

Get the temperature rising with these beautiful rusty iron candlesticks and Moroccan wall sconce. They are perfect for outdoor use too.

The ornate Mexican lantern is new but looks like it could have been lost with the Spanish Armada.

For a more Eastern or African feel, source out simple aluminium bowls or skillets and fill them with pulses, seed-pods or dried fruit.

projects

As you can clearly see opposite, for this chapter we have re-painted our floor for a third time to emulate a beautiful terracotta tiled surface, enhanced by the natural beauty of real pebbles (pages 134-5). And to this we have added a border of small 'tiles' where the reversed-out pattern is created by simple use of artists' masking-fluid (pages 130-1) – never has there been a greater testimony to the versatility of this implausible technique. We also used real pebbles to make a poor man's mosaic top for a rusty table (pages 132-3) and then created fake ones to add a bit of depth and sparkle to our wonderful sheers (pages 124-7). For our wall treatment, we discovered another way of colourwashing, where the chalky texture of the diluted layers gave a similar lustre to that of Moroccan tadlekt plaster (pages 128-9) – without nearly as much pain.

beaded muslin curtains

By the time this book is published, the world of 'sheers', or sheer fabric, will be changing – and changing rapidly: voiles, muslins and other loose-weave cotton will soon be available in a much larger range of colours and textures. Everyone is talking sheers – woven and printed patterns, and embroidered too. The rather sad offerings of the past, let's just call it 'net-city', will be usurped by a complete wealth of choice. Very beautiful and very contemporary, they are perfect for either the simple hanging or multi-layered look.

Of course, there have been some notable exceptions and the work of Tricia Guild has to be acknowledged as the leading-edge in this field, certainly in Britain. Similarly, the fabrics we've used here are exemplary. They are from a French collection L'Occitane by Elitis, who offer a sumptuous range of sheers in over thirty stunning colours.

The particular beauty of sheer fabrics is that they allow light into a room, while at the same time providing a degree of opacity and therefore privacy. They work best with simple fixings and headings. For example, on one occasion we chose to spend the budget on some expensive but delectable sheer and then simply nailed it to the window frame with shiny clout nails, using a spare one as the tieback.

Above all, sheers allow the user to be at their most creative when dressing a window, as you can see opposite and overleaf. When you look at these pictures, the question has to be asked, why choose your curtains in one colour, when you can enjoy the sheer beauty of two (pun!)? *Vive la revolution!*

MATERIALS

Muslin

Cold water or machine-wash dye

Large bucket (for cold water dye)

Rubber gloves (for cold water dye)

Modelling material in natural stone colours

Small piece of wire or large needle

Baking tray

Needle

Coloured thread

Jute string

Creating the beaded muslin curtains

Although the muslin shown here came ready-dyed in these fabulous shades, muslins and voiles are extremely easy to dye yourself, with a huge choice of colours now readily available from any haberdashers (fabric store). For the best results, use a machine-wash dye (follow the instructions carefully and it is completely safe) or a simple cold-water dye, as shown below.

If you are using muslin or other lightweight sheer material, it is a good idea to add weight to what is essentially a very thin piece of fabric - you can do this by layering or creating folds and pleats. On these curtains, we made the large flap at the top by doubling over the top hem, and then added two deep pleats at the bottom just above the hem. This helps the curtains to hang much better.

As we mentioned before, mixing colours and styles when creating curtains is very effective, too. We have enhanced ours by sewing on some decorative 'pebbles' made from modelling material that you bake in the oven, and then created a delightful beaded tassel made from jute string. The pole was made using exactly the same principle as the Skinny Sconces featured on pages 102-3. To fix the curtains to the pole, sew a few black rings to the top hem.

1 Dyeing the muslin
If you have chosen to dye your fabric, use a cold water or machine-wash dye and follow the manufacturer's instructions. For the former, you will need a large bucket.

2 Making the pebbles
Roll the modelling material in the palm of your hand into small, irregular pebble shapes and finish off each one by carefully piercing a hole at the top with the piece of wire or needle.

3 Curing the pebbles
Place the pebbles on a baking tray and bake in a hot oven for 20 to 30 minutes, according to the manufacturer's instructions, until hard. Allow them to cool completely before handling.

4 **Attaching the pebbles**
Sew the pebbles on individually with the needle and thread at regular intervals along the bottom fold of the top flap, approximately 5cm (2in) apart.

5 **Making the jute coil**
Gather the fabric and make a loop with the jute string. Lie it against the fabric and wrap the string around it to form a coil. Pull the protruding loop string taught and tie in a knot.

6 **Making the garland**
Thread some spare beads on to a piece of thread to create a 'bracelet'. Then sew the garland on to the jute string coil at the end of the curtain fabric stitching through the string.

subtle colourwash

As you might have gathered, we are great fans of colourwashing and for this room we have used a slightly different technique from that shown on pages 78-9. Still based on subtle tones, but giving a more powdery lustre, it is very suitable for this traditional two-tone scheme.

Unlike the emulsion (latex) based technique, we used our own chalky paint for the base. It contains a lot less vinyl, so is more porous, absorbing the wash much more quickly, making it less movable. The key word here is subtlety – it is essential that you dilute each wash heavily with water and make the variations between washes slight. Paint broad strokes of wash onto the wall and they will sink in to produce a lustred effect.

MATERIALS

Spirit level
Plank of wood
Drapers' chalk
Water-based paints in Barley,
Fresco Pink and New England Red
At least two very weak
colourwashes in Mustard and
Adobe Red
Large paint brush
Masking tape
Soft stencil brush
Medium grade wire wool

1 Creating the half-and-half
Use the level, plank and chalk to draw a line one third of the way up the wall. Paint the top Barley and when dry apply a Mustard wash, then a stronger wash. Paint the lower section Fresco Pink.

2 Adding the washes
Use the weakest Adobe Red wash first. Brush it on with broad strokes, first one way then another, working your way up and down the wall, making sure to brush in any drips. Allow to dry and repeat with a stronger wash.

3 Creating the border
Mark lines with masking tape on the dividing line and approximately 2.5cm (1in) below it. Then stipple on New England Red with the stencil brush between the tapes and, when dry, rub back with wire wool.

paint resist tiles

These paint 'resist' tiles are vaguely reminiscent of what the ceramic world call slipware, where a transparent slip is used to create a raised glaze or pattern. Here, our designs are reversed-out so you see the base colour below and they certainly have the three-dimensional quality of slipware.

This project introduces a wonderful accessory for creating resists - artists' masking fluid. It is similar in use to latex-based household glue, but due to its lighter consistency it is easier to use and to remove, and it dries much more quickly. Also, it is a lot more controllable, so precise patterns can be painted easily. But, don't leave it too long - 48 hours maximum.

So as not to harm your painted tiles, as with the tiled floor, use real tilers' grout that comes in powder form, rather than the ready-mixed variety.

MATERIALS

MDF 'tiles' cut to size and edges softened with medium sandpaper
Water-based paints in Buttermilk and New England Red
Masking fluid
Artists' paint brush
Acrylic dead-flat (satin) varnish

1 Painting the tiles
Apply two coats of Buttermilk and leave to dry. Paint on the designs with masking fluid.

2 Painting the top coat
After a few minutes, the masking fluid will be dry and you can then apply a top coat of New England Red to the tiles.

3 Completing the tiles
When the paint is dry, remove the fluid by gently rubbing the design. Apply two coats of varnish, including the sides.

simnel cake table top

The Moroccans have a tradition known as tadlekt, a lime-dust plastering technique most frequently used on walls that has a beautiful lustre. But again the process is lengthy, so you will be relieved to hear that our Simnel Cake Table Top, while not quite in the same league as tadlekt, does give a flat and pleasing surface to a table. With the subtlety of a colourwash on top, it is a passable alternative. And even better, it takes just minutes to achieve.

Levelling compound is quite brilliant stuff and is normally used as a skim coat to make concrete floors flat and level. But it must not be more than 3mm ($1/8$in) thick on each coating and with a shelf-life of only 15 minutes when mixed, you do have to work quickly!

MATERIALS
5kg (11lb) levelling compound
Table
Straight edge
Pebbles 20-30mm ($3/4$-$1 1/4$in) diameter, washed and dried
Small trowel or palette knife
Acrylic dead-flat (satin) varnish
Water-based paint in Barley
Colourwash in Mustard (diluted minimum 50:50 water:paint)
5cm (2in) paint brush

1 Applying the compound
Mix the levelling compound following the pack's guidelines. Ensure there are no lumps, and then pour the compound on to the table. Use the edge to wipe off excess.

2 Placing the pebbles
Having pre-sorted sufficient pebbles, simply press them firmly into the levelling compound, working quickly around the table. Flatten any ridges with a small trowel and leave overnight.

3 Finishing off
Apply a good coat of varnish and when dry, paint on two coats of Barley, followed by one or two washes of Mustard. Finish off with two more coats of the dead-flat (satin) varnish.

pebble border

This is, of course, another Faux Stone Floor, made exactly as on pages 40-3. In terms of authentic appearance, it is probably the most successful, but ironically it is the easiest to replicate. The tiles are merely painted with our terracotta paint and with the hue left from the excess grout, they take on a resemblance to terracotta that is almost beyond belief.

The pebble-border is real however. It's an idea that could be used both inside and out and as the pebbles merely sit in the dry mortar before adding the water, no arduous mixing, or mixer, is required. Take great care when adding the water to the mortar; you must ensure that the edges of the tiles are varnished and well-protected by the plastic sheeting. For the materials and method for creating the Faux Stone Floor see pages 40-3.

MATERIALS
Masking tape
Plastic sheeting
Large bucket
Sharp sand and cement
(ready-mixed if possible)
Trowel
Pebbles 10-20mm ($\frac{1}{2}$-$\frac{3}{4}$in) diameter, washed and dried
Water spray with fine nozzle

1 Preparing the cement
Mask off the channel left by the tiles with masking tape and the plastic and fill with the dry mixed cement. Level and flatten with the trowel.

2 Laying the pebbles
Press the pebbles neatly and firmly into the dry mortar; they need to be lodged well into the cement powder. Brush additional dry cement over the finished surface.

3 Wetting the mortar
Use the water spray to wet the surface thoroughly, avoiding any exposed tiles where possible. As the cement absorbs the water, it will set hard.

Fabric paints

The fabric paints used in this book are based on printing inks and use a base medium and are also available through Grand Illusions. This extends the paint, but without losing its density of colour - it is this that allows you to paint large quantities of fabric without much ink. Beware: not all fabric paints perform in this manner.

• Mix two tsps of paint to 300ml (10fl oz) of Base Medium. Then add a little water and mix thoroughly until you have the consistency of single cream. This should be sufficient for 2-3m (2-3yds) of fabric.

• When using the paint to stamp patterns, use less water so that the consistency is more like double cream.

• When creating colours by mixing the paints, make a base colour as above, but always add the mixing colours diluted in water first. This allows you to create tints slowly and gently.

• Always experiment first with very small quantities until you find the correct tone. Light colours will not register on top of dark backgrounds.

• When dry, fix with a hot iron - this will allow the fabric to be washable.

And finally...

Both our Traditional Paints and the new Fabric Paints are available by mail-order - see the address in the list of stockists, on pages 140-1.

In most of the projects in the book there are terms in brackets - these apply to the US market only.

suppliers

Paints and varnishes

Grand Illusions
2-4 Crown Road
St Margarets
Twickenham
Middlesex TW1 3EE
UK
Tel: 0181 892 2151
Shops and Maison mail-
order catalogue
(*new generation water-
based paints, fabric
paints, acrylic varnishes,
cold patinating fluid,
furniture supplied natural
ready for painting*)

Craig and Rose plc
172 Leith Walk
Edinburgh EH6 5ER
UK
Tel: 0131 554 1131
(*paints and varnishes*)

Paint Magic
116 Sheen Road
Richmond
Surrey TW9 1UR
UK

Tel: 0181 940 5503
(*paints and varnishes;
their woodwash is similar
to Grand Illusions paint*)

Relics of Witney
35 Bridge Street
Witney
Oxon OX8 6DA
UK
Tel: 01993 704611
(*Colourman Paints, which
are also available from
other specialist paint
shops all around the
country*)

Createx Colors
14 Airport Park Road
East Granby
CT 06026
USA
Tel: 800 243 2712
(*colouring agents for most
surfaces, including
pearlescents, iridescents,
acrylics, fabric colours,
pure pigments, liquid
dyes*)

Old-Fashioned Milk Paint Co
PO Box 222
Grolon
MA 01450
USA
Tel: 617 448 6336
(*powder milk paints*)

Paint Effects
2426 Fillmore Street
San Francisco
CA 94115
USA
Tel: 415 292 7780
(*Paint Magic woodwash
colours and other supplies*)

Fabrics

IKEA
Branches throughout the
UK. Phone for nearest
branch.
Tel: 0181 451 5566

John Lewis Partnership
Branches throughout the
UK. Phone for nearest
branch.
Tel: 0171 828 1000

Russell & Chapple
23 Monmouth Street
London WC2H 9DE
UK
Tel: 0171 836 7521

Muriel Short Designs
Hewitts Estate
Elmbridge Road, Cranleigh
Surrey GU6 8LW
UK
Tel: 01483 271211
(*UK importer for French
muslins*)

Coconut Company
129-131 Greene Street
New York
NY 10012
USA
Tel: 212 539 1940

Homespun Fabrics &
Draperies
PO Box 3223
Ventura
CA 93006
USA
Tel: 805 642 8111

IKEA
1000 Center Drive
Elizabeth
NJ 07202
USA
Tel: 908 289 4488

Natural Fiber Fabric Club
PO Box 1115
Mountainside
NJ 07092
USA

Decorative trims
Jali (UK) Ltd
Apsley House
Chartham
Canterbury
Kent CT4 7HT
UK
Tel: 01227 831710
(*call for details of
stockists*)

General supplies
B&Q
Branches throughout the
UK. Phone for nearest
branch.

(*good for pre-cut timber
and brass/zinc tubing,
plumbing supplies*)

Homebase
Branches throughout the UK
(*good for pre-cut timber
etc*)

The Artist's Club
5750 N.E. Hassalo
Portland
OR 97213
USA
Tel: 800 845 6507
(*craft painting materials
and supplies, including a
wide selection of paints
and brushes*)

Chaselle Inc
9645 Gerwig Lane
Columbia
MD 2104
USA
Tel: 800 242 7355
(*brushes, paints, tempera
colors, acrylics, pastels,
and other crafts supplies*)

index